Violin Method for Beginners

Book 1

By: Jamie Chimchirian

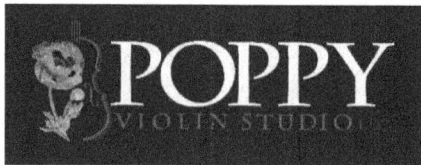

www.poppyviolinstudio.com

Contents

How to Use this Book

The goal of this book is to provide beginner violin students with a solid understanding of basic techniques and note reading. The curriculum is easy to follow, provides simple visual diagrams and detailed explanations of new techniques. Concepts are introduced gradually so students can master new techniques one at a time. Each section provides targeted exercises and songs to reinforce lesson material. With a mission of making quality violin instruction accessible, author and violinist Dr. Jamie Chimchirian offers a completely free YouTube tutorial series to accompany all exercises and songs found in this book. After completing all 27 lessons and tutorials, students will be able to read music and play songs that incorporate the use of all four fingers on the strings.

Each song in this book has a series of accompanying chord symbols. Common accompaniment instruments include guitar and piano. You will hear examples of these accompaniments in the recordings provided in YouTube lessons 13, 21 and 27. Below is a glossary of the accompaniment chords used for the songs in these lessons.

AM= A major chord
A7= A major or A dominant 7th chord
Bm= B minor chord
BM= B major chord
B7= B major or B dominant 7th chord
C#m= C sharp minor chord
DM= D major chord
EM= E major chord
E7=E major or E dominant 7th chord
F#m= F sharp minor chord
GM= G major chord
G#m= G sharp minor chord

To access the accompanying YouTube videos, look for the QR code and website link on each lesson page.

YouTube Channel: Jamie Chimchirian

Playlist: Violin Method for Beginners

https://youtube.com/playlist?list=PLTaAxpCJaIGkI9T0n-GJ_lLxUf7Xjq-42

INTRODUCTION

In this section you will learn the following:

1. The Parts of the Violin and Bow

2. How to Tune the Violin

3. How to Hold the Violin

4. How to Hold the Bow

LESSON 1: The Parts of the Violin and Bow

https://youtu.be/TbfOxE3Y_H8

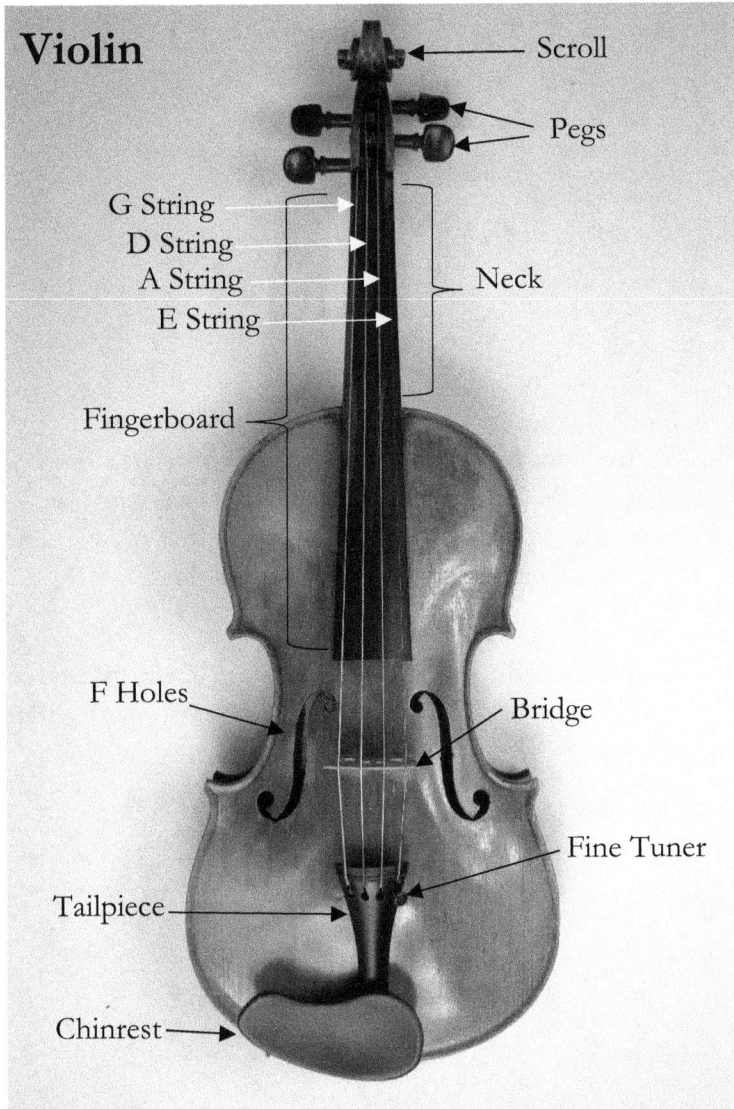

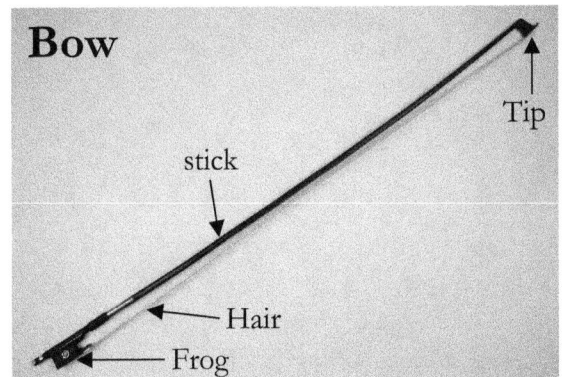

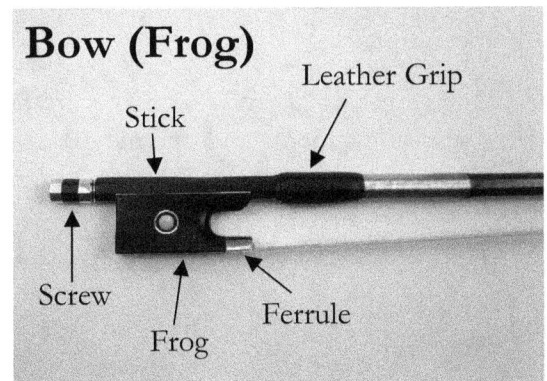

Violin

- Scroll
- Pegs
- G String
- D String
- A String
- E String
- Neck
- Fingerboard
- F Holes
- Bridge
- Fine Tuner
- Tailpiece
- Chinrest

Bow

- Tip
- stick
- Hair
- Frog

Bow (Frog)

- Leather Grip
- Stick
- Screw
- Frog
- Ferrule

Scan the QR code beside the Lesson 1 title to learn more about the different parts of the violin and bow, and some basic violin and bow maintenance.

LESSON 2: How to Tune the Violin

https://youtu.be/nsWBIkq1pOE

The Four Violin Strings:

E String

A String

D String

G String

To tune the violin strings, make sure that you have access to a tuner that is set to the standard tuning pitch of A, set specifically to the frequency of 440 hertz. This is abbreviated in musical terms as A=440. Tuning devices can be found in various forms, including battery operated tuners, cell phone apps and tuning forks. Unless you already have a honed musical ear, you will need to use a tuner for each string. The violin should be tuned before every practice session or performance.

The pegs and fine tuners are the two ways to tune the strings on the violin. The pegs are for larger adjustments and the fine tuners are for smaller adjustments. When the string becomes tighter, the pitch will rise, and when it is looser, the pitch will fall.

Scan the QR code beside the Lesson 2 title for the tutorial on how to tune the violin.

LESSON 3: How to Hold the Violin

https://youtu.be/N3939letlSQ

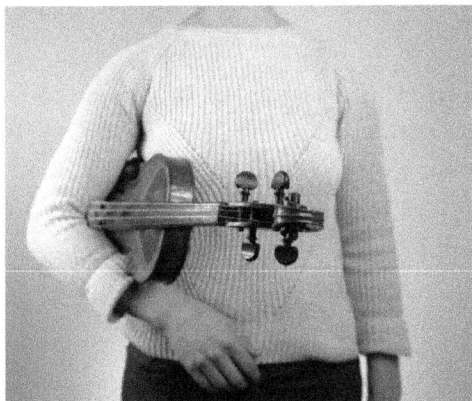

Rest Position: Violin held securely under right elbow just behind bridge.

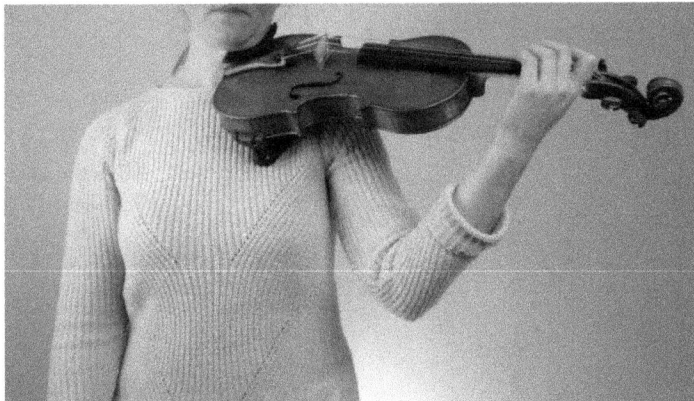

Playing Position: Violin placed on left shoulder and held in place by dropping left jaw onto chinrest.

Rest Position and Playing Position

Learning healthy posture is one of the most basic and important techniques in violin playing. There are two main positions for holding the violin: **rest position** and **playing position**, as shown in the figure above. Rest position is when the violin is held between the right ribs and the right elbow. Playing position is when the violin is placed on the left shoulder so it can be played. Scan the QR code beside the Lesson 3 title to watch the tutorial on how to hold the violin.

While holding the violin in playing position, the tailpiece should be pointed towards your throat, and the violin should significantly cover your left shoulder. Many beginners are tempted to hold the violin too far forward because they want to watch their left-hand fingers, but this encourages poor posture. The violin should be held parallel to the floor so make sure to avoid drooping the scroll downwards. If the violin is slipping off your shoulder, your neck feels strained, or it is simply uncomfortable, it is recommended that you use a sponge or a shoulder rest to lift the violin up off the shoulder and to help avoid unnecessary strain.

The left hand is placed at the very end of the neck of the violin, with the thumb on the G string side, and the fingers on the E string side. Be careful not to clench the neck of the violin between the thumb and fingers.

EXERCISE 3

Practice the transition from rest position to playing position five times in a row. Repeat this for several weeks so you can work on good posture before you begin playing on the violin in later lessons.

LESSON 4: How to Hold the Bow

https://youtu.be/JHlE6f6U7GQ

Two Versions of the Bow Hold

There are two versions of the bow hold that you will learn in this lesson: the **beginner bow hold** and the **traditional bow hold.** The difference between the two is the placement of the thumb. Beginners who start with the beginner bow hold will eventually start using the traditional bow hold when they are ready. As a general suggestion, young children should start by using the beginner bow hold because it makes it easier for them to place the other fingers correctly. Scan the QR code beside the Lesson 4 title for a detailed video lesson on how to hold the bow.

Traditional Bow Hold

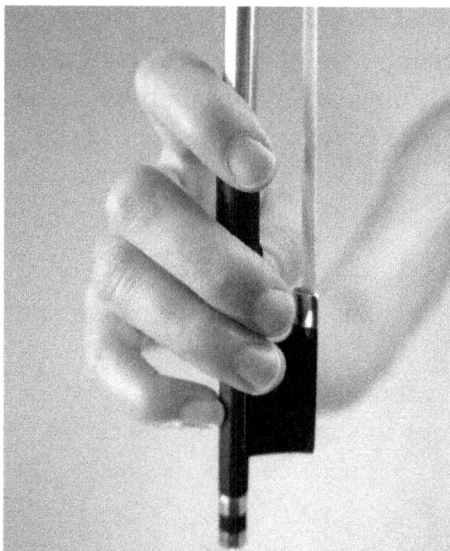

Beginner Bow Hold

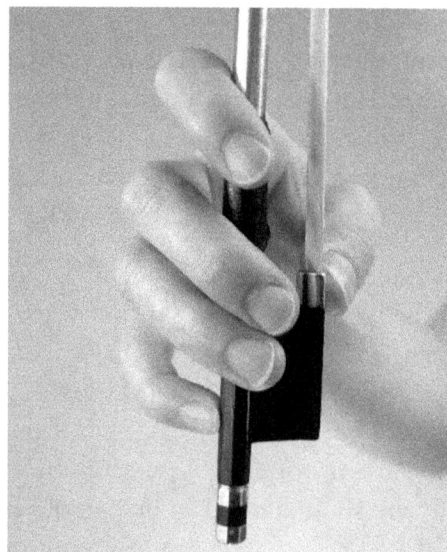

Traditional Bow Hold

The **thumb** should be placed on the bare wood of the stick, just above the frog and just below the leather winding. Do not put the thumb inside the U-shaped space inside the frog. The thumb should contact the stick just beneath the nail on the fingertip of the thumb so that it can bend and straighten as needed. Rigidity in the thumb often stems from incorrect thumb placement and produces a rigid tone.

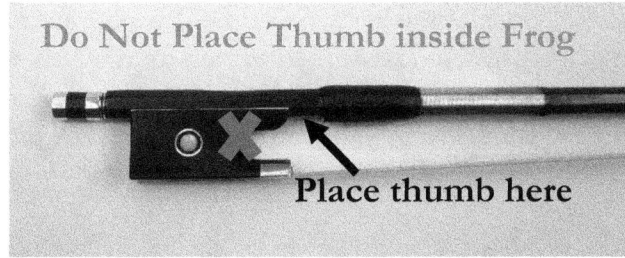

Do Not Place Thumb inside Frog

Place thumb here

Correct: Thumb placed on tip

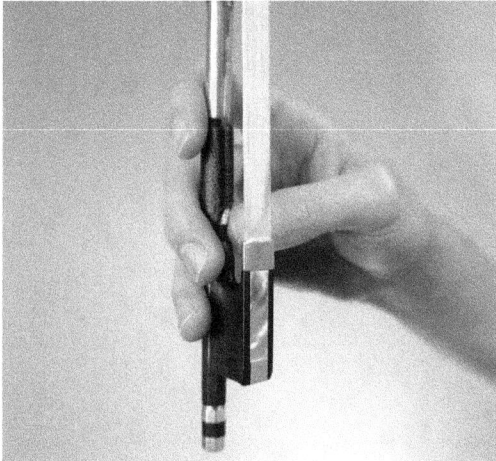

Incorrect: Thumb protruding

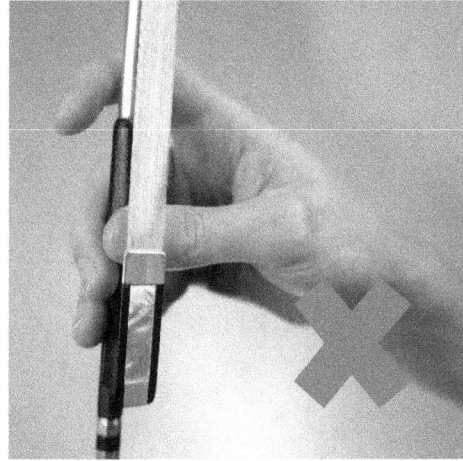

The **ring finger** and **middle finger** should wrap gently around the frog at a slight diagonal. Using the finger pad, the ring finger should contact the center of the frog. The middle finger pad will contact the frog just above the ring finger.

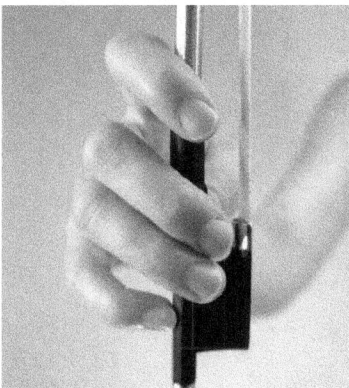

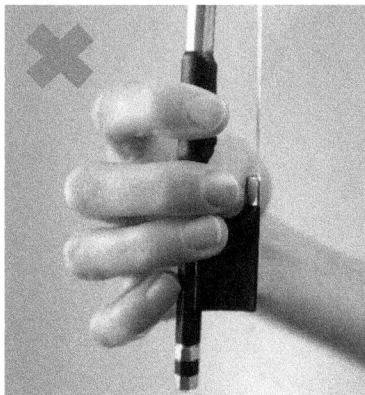

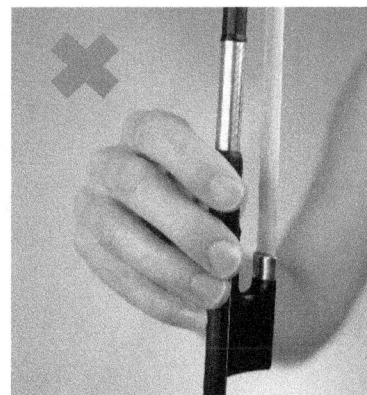

Correct:
Middle and ring finger angled with finger pads touching frog

Incorrect:
Middle and ring fingers placed perpendicular to frog

Incorrect:
Middle and ring fingers bunched together and not touching frog

11

The **pinky finger** should contact the bare stick at the base of the frog. Only the fingertip of the pinky finger should contact the stick, and it should remain round. This will take some practice as the pinky finger is the weakest of all the fingers and it will need constant attention in the beginning to ensure that it maintains this posture. Watch out for the dreaded "stick pinky" where the pinky is eternally stuck in a straight line with no bend in the knuckles. To avoid this, make sure the other fingers are placed correctly.

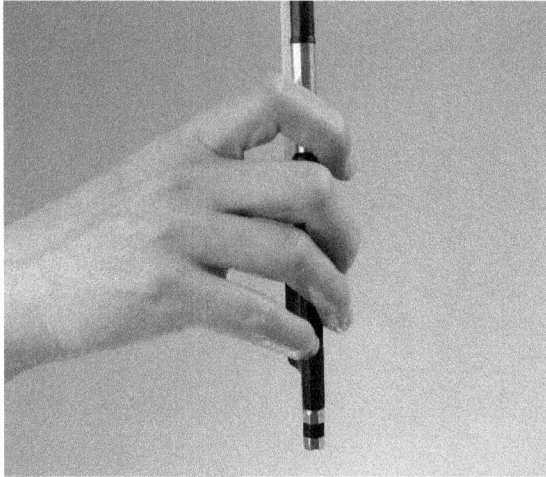

Correct: Pinky round, fingers and thumb gently rounded

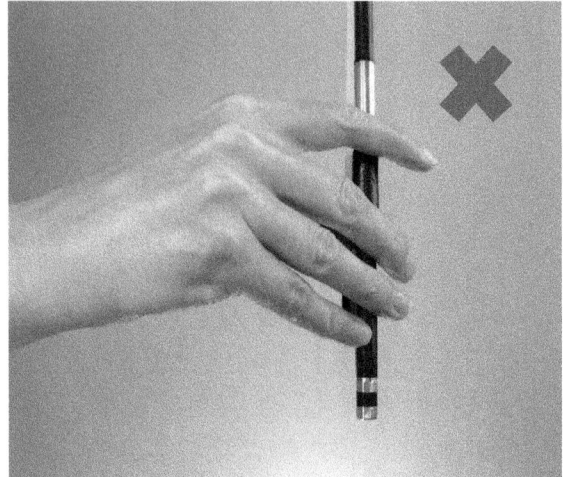

Incorrect: "Stick pinky", fingers and thumb straight and rigid

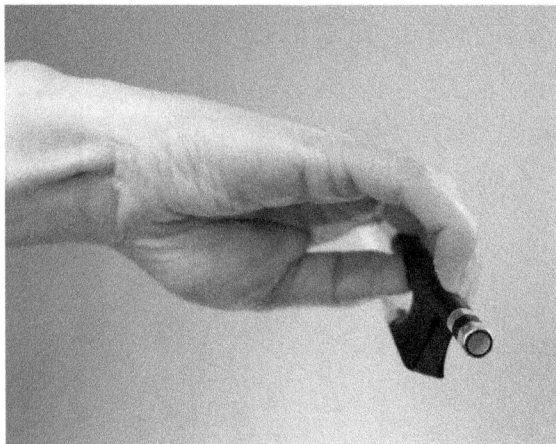

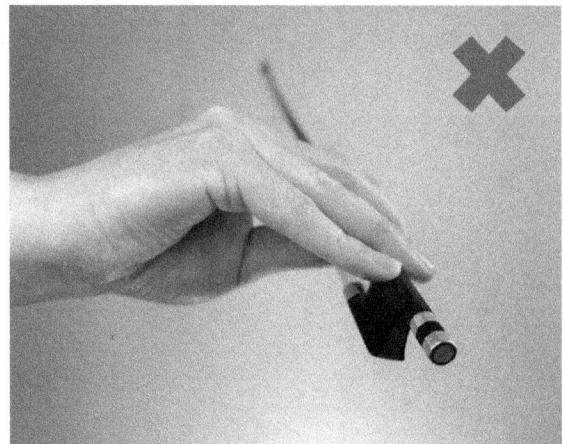

The **index finger** should contact the bow where the leather portion of the stick meets the silver winding. Place the index finger on its side, in between the middle knuckle and the nail.

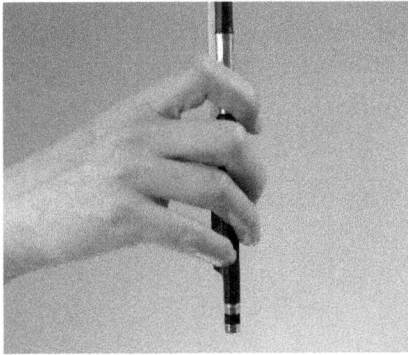

Correct: Index finger resting easily on silver winding between middle joint and nail.

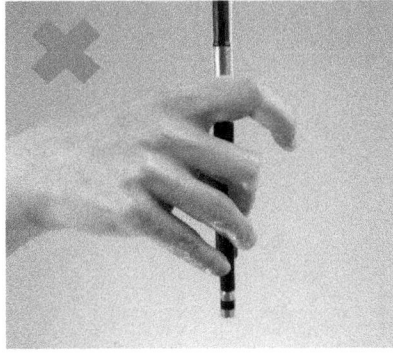

Incorrect: Index finger contacting too close to base joint.

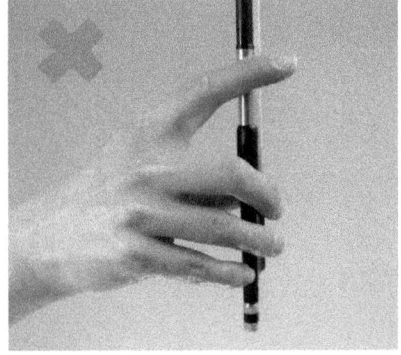

Incorrect: Too much space between index and middle finger.

Beginner Bow Hold

Thumb placement is the only difference between the traditional bow hold and the beginner bow hold. Follow the descriptions for the ring, middle, pinky and index finger placements that are described in the previous section.

The thumb should contact the silver ferrule, located where the bow hair meets the frog. The thumb should be able to bend and straighten freely.

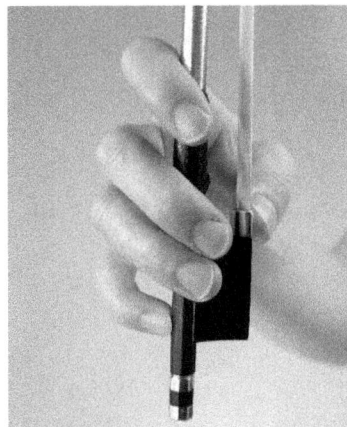

Beginner Bow Hold

EXCERCISE 4

Practice making the bow hold five to ten times in a row. Repeat this daily for four to eight weeks so you can build necessary strength in your finger and hand muscles as you start playing on the violin in later lessons.

SECTION 1

In this section you will learn the following:

1. How to play six notes on the violin, including first finger and second finger notes

2. An introduction on how to read music

3. How to play and read four rhythms, including quarter notes, eighth notes and sixteenth notes

4. Songs that combine all rhythms and notes from this section.

LESSON 5: Reading E String and A String

https://youtu.be/odoAMgXcBwc

Violin music uses the **Treble Clef.** The **Staff** is made up of five lines and four spaces. Each space and line has a specific letter name. E and A are both "space notes", or notes that fall in a space. Notice how **E** is in the top space on the staff, and **A** is in the third space from the top. The numbers listed immediately to the right of the treble clef are the **time signature**. Time signatures will be explored in greater detail in Lesson 18. All notes written in the following exercises are **quarter notes**. Quarter notes will be explained further in lesson 6.

The first two pitches that you will learn to play on the violin are **E** and **A**. These pitches are played with open E string and open A string. "Open" means that you will not be pressing any left-hand fingers down.

Scan the QR code beside the Lesson 5 title to watch the tutorial on how to read E and A.

EXERCISE 5
Practice saying the names of the notes in each line
of music below. Say "E" when you see an open E
string and say "A" when you see an open A string.

5. E String and A String

Chimchirian

16

LESSON 6: Flower Garden Rhythms 1

https://youtu.be/Iv1agfRxlBg

Learning Rhythms with Words

In this lesson, you will learn four flower garden rhythms: **Poppy, Honeysuckle, Sunflower** and **Rose.** These rhythms are made up of eighth notes, sixteenth notes and quarter notes. Scan the QR code beside the Lesson 6 title to watch the tutorial for these rhythms.

Poppy

This is a Quarter Rest

rest   rest

Pop-py   Pop-py

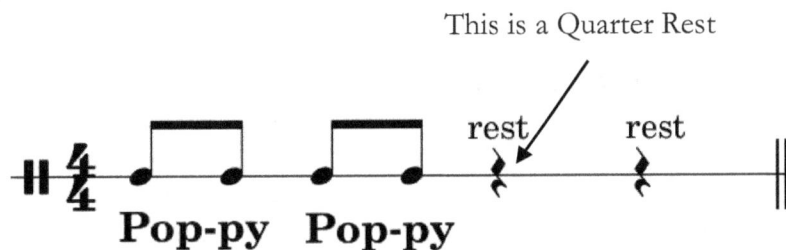

Each Poppy rhythm is two **eighth notes**. You will normally see eighth notes beamed together with one solid bar connecting them in groups of two, or sometimes four.

Honeysuckle

rest   rest

hon - ey - suc- kle   hon - ey - suc - kle

Each Honeysuckle rhythm is four **sixteenth notes**. You will normally see sixteenth notes beamed together in groups of four. Notice how sixteenth notes have two lines (beams) on top. This is how you can tell them apart from eighth notes, which only have one line (beam) on top.

Sunflower

Each Sunflower rhythm is a combination of one **eighth note** and two **sixteenth notes**. Notice how the eighth note has one beam and the sixteenth notes have two beams.

Rose

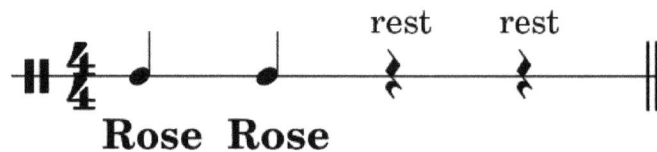

Each Rose rhythm is one **quarter note**. Notice how quarter notes do not have any beams. Quarter notes are longer in duration than eighth notes and sixteenth notes and equal one count or beat.

Understanding Note Durations

In this book, you will use quarter notes as the basic metric unit.

A quarter note equals one beat, or count.

An eighth note is equal to half of a quarter note, so two eighth notes equal one quarter note.

A sixteenth note is a quarter of a beat, so four sixteenth notes fit into one quarter note.

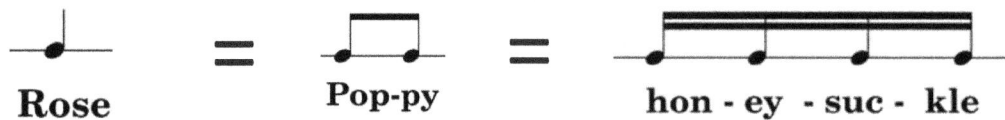

One quarter note   =   Two eighth notes   =   Four sixteenth notes

Rests

A **rest** indicates that you will stop playing for a specific amount of time. Notice there are two rests following each flower garden rhythm. These are called **quarter rests**, and just like quarter notes, they each equal one beat.

$\large\xi$ Quarter Rest

PRACTICE TIP!

The rests following each flower garden rhythm will allow you to build control and rhythmic accuracy. When you start physically playing the violin, **these rests become very important**. While it may be tempting to leave them out, understand that they are included to help you learn new techniques thoroughly and efficiently.

EXERCISE 6
Practice clapping and saying each of the flower garden rhythms until you feel that you have internalized them.

Now, it's time to play the violin!

LESSON 7: Playing on E String

https://youtu.be/qViA8mNmCTw

Using the Bow

Understanding the following concepts will help you succeed while using the bow on the string. Scan the QR code beside the Lesson 7 title to watch the tutorial about using the bow on the E string.

Bowings

You will notice two symbols above some of the notes at the beginning of each line. These are called **bowings**, and they will remind you which direction your bow should be moving.

Down Bow: means that the bow is moving towards the floor

Up Bow: means the bow is moving towards the sky

*When bowings are not written, continue playing the same bowing pattern until otherwise indicated

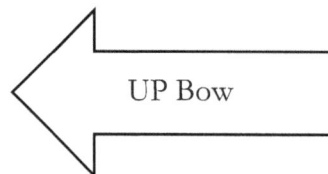

Bow Placement

Before you are ready to play, place your bow on the string at the **middle** of the bow. Most likely, your right elbow will be bent at a ninety-degree angle. This is where you should place the bow before playing most of the exercises and songs in this book. Try adhering a sticker or thin piece of tape to the stick of the bow, right at the middle, to serve as a visual aid while practicing.

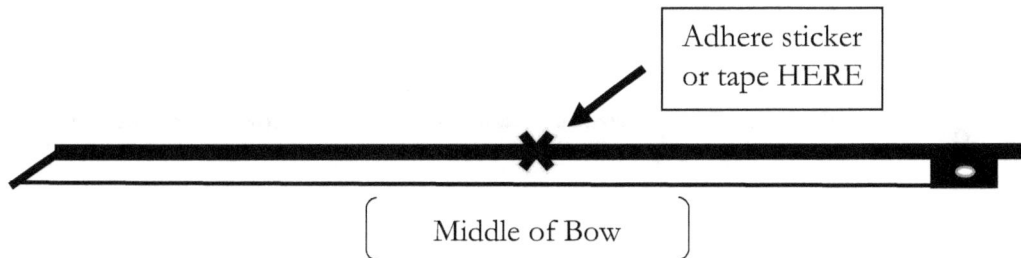

Adhere sticker or tape HERE

Middle of Bow

Contact Point on String

Contact point refers to the point where the bow touches the string. The bow can be placed on the string anywhere between the bridge and the end of the fingerboard, but for beginners, it is best to stay in the **middle lane**, or the part of the string that is even with the top of the f holes. It is important to keep the bow in one lane for good tone production. As you start playing, work on keeping your bow in the middle lane on the string. Do not allow the bow to move over the fingerboard or the bridge.

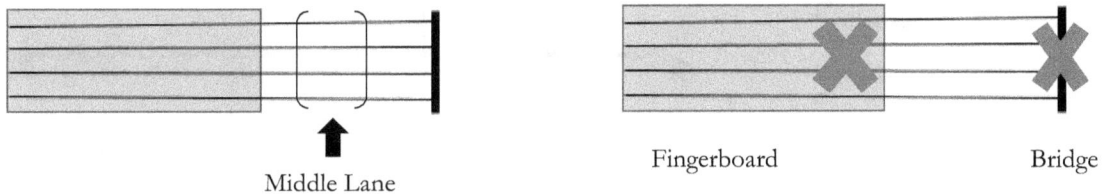

Middle Lane

Fingerboard   Bridge

Straight Bow

Playing with a **straight bow**, one where the bow is parallel with the bridge is the basis of good bow technique. Practice facing a mirror while you play and watch that your bow stays parallel to the bridge. If you play with **crooked bow**, it will be difficult to control your bow and to create good sound.

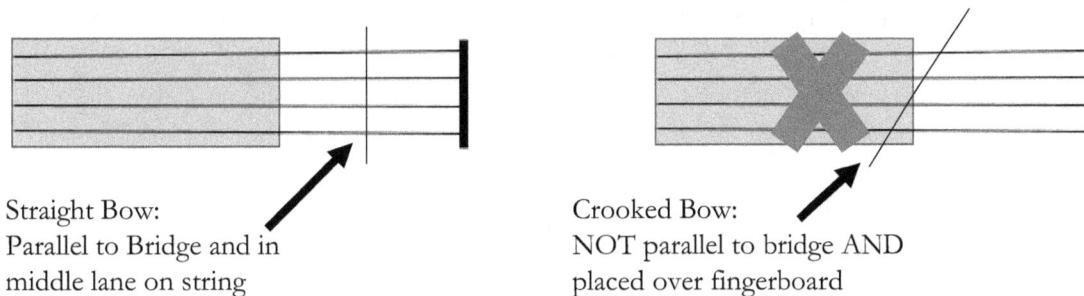

Straight Bow:
Parallel to Bridge and in
middle lane on string

Crooked Bow:
NOT parallel to bridge AND
placed over fingerboard

Amount of Bow

It is helpful to determine the **amount of bow** that is necessary for each rhythm. Longer and slower notes, like quarter notes, will need a longer bow stroke, while shorter and quicker notes, like sixteenth notes, will use considerably smaller bow strokes. The arrows below indicate the amount of bow that should be used for each rhythm.

1. Rose

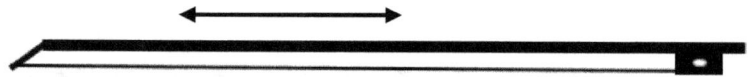

2. Poppy

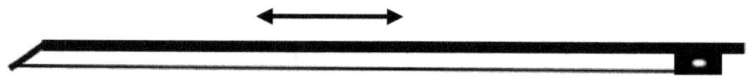

3. Honeysuckle

 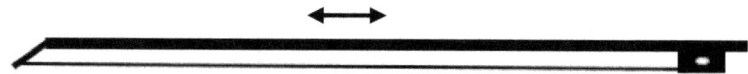

4. Sunflower

 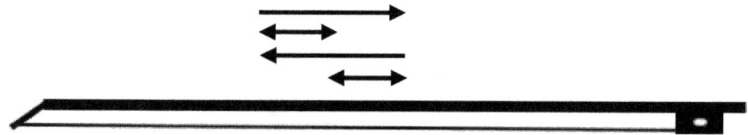

EXERCISE 7
Practice playing each flower garden rhythm on the E string. Remember to place your bow on the string at the middle of the bow, in the middle lane on the string and work on keeping a straight bow as you play. Continue practicing these exercises until you can play them smoothly with good sound.

7. Flower Garden Rhythms 1

Chimchirian

"Poppy" on E String

*Repeat sign means to
play the line one more time

"Honeysuckle" on E String

"Sunflower" on E String

*Staccato Dots

"Rose" on E String

*Dots written directly above or below a notehead indicate "staccato".
Staccato is an articulation that means to play each note short and detached.

Staccato and other articulations will be discussed in more detail in lesson 24.

23

LESSON 8: String Crossings

https://youtu.be/3C-XKTg4MGI

Changing from E string to A string

The "**Rock n Roll**" exercise, practices moving the bow from one string to another. Start by placing your bow on the E string and practice silently "rocking" the bow over to the A string by slightly lifting your right elbow. Then try lowering your elbow just enough to "roll" back to the E string. String crossing is a crucial skill that will help you develop the control necessary to play on only one string at a time. Beginners who do not take enough time to master string crossings will often end up accidentally playing more than one string as they play.

In exercise 8, use the "Rock n Roll" motion to play the flower garden rhythms on both E string and A string. Scan the QR code beside the lesson 8 title to watch the tutorial video on how to change strings.

Practice playing each flower garden rhythm on E string and A string.
Remember to place your bow on the string at the middle of the bow, in the
middle lane on the string and work on keeping a straight bow as you play.

8. Rock n' Roll

"Poppy" Rock n' Roll

"Honeysuckle" Rock n' Roll

"Sunflower" Rock n' Roll

"Rose" Rock n' Roll

LESSON 9: The First Finger

https://youtu.be/CgcNCNrpOoo

Playing the First Finger on A string and E string

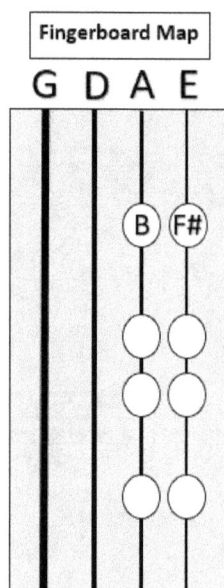

Fingerboard Map

G D A E

(B) (F#)

The left-hand index finger is referred to as the **first finger**. You will use the fingertip of your first finger to press down the string in a precise location to play two new notes: B and F#. Scan the QR code beside the lesson 9 title to watch the tutorial on how to play and read first finger. The hashtag symbol (#) used in music notation is called a **sharp**.

B
is played with first finger on A string, or 1 on A

F# ("F sharp")
is played with first finger on E String, or 1 on E

Reading First Finger on A String and E String

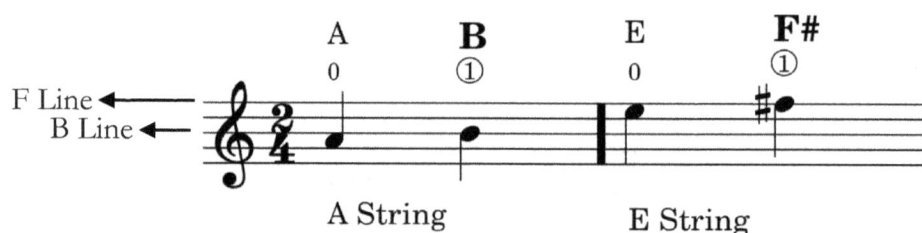

A
0

B
①

E
0

F#
①

F Line ←
B Line ←

A String   E String

When viewing the music above, notice how each of these first finger notes are notes that fall on a line. **B** is on the middle line, or the line just above the space for A, indicating that it is one step higher. The same happens for **F#**: it occupies the top line, just above the E space.

Intonation of the First Finger

Intonation is the term used to describe the accuracy of a pitch. It can be challenging when first learning the violin to play **in tune**, or with proper intonation. The best way to cultivate good intonation is to work on building strong listening skills. Listening to recordings, watching tutorials, and singing are all excellent ways to build a strong ear. Using the YouTube tutorials included with this book will help you develop a strong sense of pitch. If you learn what notes sound like, then you can find the correct place for the first finger on the A string and E string.

Finger Tapes?

Some teachers find it helpful to aid beginners by adhering tapes to the fingerboard, like frets on a guitar. Placed correctly, these tapes provide a visual marker for the left-hand fingers that can help aid beginners. These tapes are a supplement, not a requirement, and are not a replacement for building strong listening skills.

Adjusting for Proper Intonation

As you begin to use your left-hand fingers to press down the strings, listen carefully to the pitch that you create. Your ear is the best guide for learning how to adjust a finger that is out of tune. You want the pitch you create to match the one you are hearing on the tutorial. If you can, identify if the out of tune note is too high or too low and move your fingertip to correct your intonation. Be patient, especially in the beginning.

Eventually you will build "muscle memory" and your fingers will know where to press down the string with much less effort.

EXERCISE 9

While playing each flower garden rhythm, practice putting down your first finger on E string to create F# and on A string to create B. To learn what F# and B sound like, watch the lesson 9 YouTube tutorial. Listen carefully and adjust the placement of your fingertip if you are not playing in tune.

9. The First Finger

*The **Key Signature** is a collection of accidentals listed at the beginning of a piece of music and indicates specific pitches that will be altered in the music. In this example, there are 3 accidentals, specifically, 3 sharps, including F#, which means the music is written in the Key of A Major. A detailed explanation of key signatures is beyond the scope of the material covered in this book.

"Rose" on E String

"Rose" on A String

LESSON 10: The Second Finger

https://youtu.be/Qt6rs-GzeoY

Playing the Second Finger on A String and E String

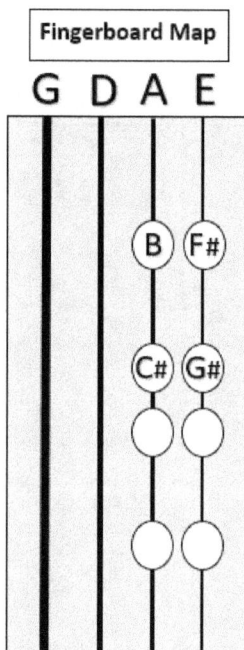

The left-hand middle finger is referred to as the **second finger**. You will use the fingertip of your second finger to press down the string in a precise location to play two new pitches, C# and G#. Scan the QR code beside the Lesson 10 title to watch the tutorial on how to play second finger.

C# ("C Sharp")	**G#** ("G Sharp")
which is played with second finger on A string, or 2 on A	which is played with second finger on E String, or 2 on E

Reading the Second Finger on A String and E String

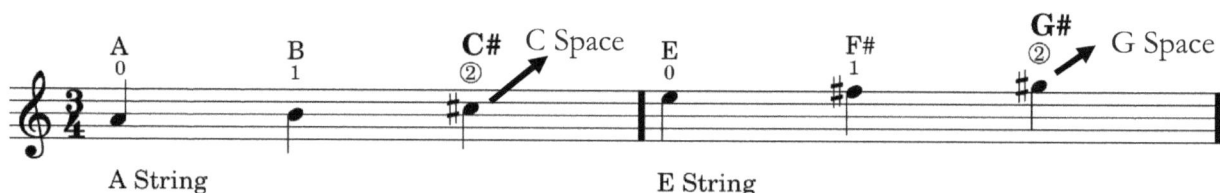

When viewing the music above, notice how each of these second finger notes both fall in spaces between the lines. **C#** is in the second space from the top of the staff, or the space just above the line for B, indicating that it is one step higher. The same happens for **G#**: it occupies the space above the staff, just above the F# line.

30

While playing the flower garden rhythms, practice pressing down the first finger on E string to make F#, and then the second finger to make **G#**. You will also practice putting down the first finger on A string, to make B, and then the second finger to make **C#**. To learn what G# and C# sound like, watch the lesson 10 tutorial. Listen carefully and adjust the placement of your fingertip if you are not playing in tune.

10. The Second Finger

"Sunflower" on E String

"Sunflower" on A String

"Rose" on E String

"Rose" on A String

SUPPLEMENT: The 4-Step Practice Method

The Importance of Practicing Slowly

When learning the songs in this book, make sure to **practice slowly.** Going slowly allows the mind and body to absorb new concepts thoroughly and deeply. This process cannot be rushed and attempting to do so can result in poor habits and frustration.

The 4-Step Practice Method

While learning new songs, follow this **4-step practice method.**

1. Learn the Notes
2. Learn the Rhythms
3. Play Slowly with the Violin and Bow
4. Repeat Until Smooth

Step 1: Know the Notes

Practice this step without the violin.

Study the music and make sure that you can identify every note. Is it an open A or a C#? A first finger or second finger and on which string? Practice saying or singing the note names for each song with the accompanying YouTube recording to make sure you have completed this step.

Step 2: Learn the Rhythms

Practice this step without the violin.

Study the music and make sure you know all the rhythms. Practice clapping the rhythms for each song with the accompanying YouTube recording so that you have internalized them before moving on to step 3.

Step 3: Play Slowly on the Violin

Now that you thoroughly know the notes and rhythms in your mind, you can start playing on the violin. Remember to go slowly and be patient. You will make mistakes and that is a normal part of the learning process.

Step 4: Repeat Until Smooth

Slow and focused repetitions during practice sessions are the secret ingredient for smooth performances. Continue playing through a line or song slowly, at least 5 times in a row, until it starts to flow more easily. Depending on the difficulty of the piece and how frequently you practice, this process may take several weeks. Once you can play a song easily and smoothly at a slow tempo, you can gradually speed up the tempo to play it faster.

Now it is time to start playing some music!

https://youtu.be/kYCKKJinvbA

EXERCISE 11

Scan the QR code beside the Lesson 11 title to watch the tutorial for Mary Had a Little Lamb.
You can also use the 4-step practice method to learn this song.

11. Mary Had a Little Lamb

Chord Symbols (see page 4)

Traditional Arr. Chimchirian

The two dots written just before the
final bar line are a **repeat sign**.
Repeat the song one more time.

https://youtu.be/9PtI92CV_NY

EXERCISE 12

Scan the QR code beside the Lesson 12 title to watch the tutorial for the Honeysuckle Vine. You can also use the 4-step practice method to learn this song.

12. The Honeysuckle Vine

J. Chimchirian

https://youtu.be/CSqKCrKxMik

EXERCISE 13

Scan the QR code beside the Lesson 13 title to listen to the songs in Lesson 13. Use the 4-step practice method from Lesson 7 to learn the songs in lesson 13 on your own.

13a: Hot Cross Buns

Traditional Arr. Chimchirian

The "Circle Bow" or "Retake"

Sometimes while playing, it is necessary to change the standard "down up down up" bowing pattern. A **circle bow** or **retake** is used when it is necessary to play two down bows in a row.

To complete a circle bow, finish the first down bow, then continue moving the bow in a counterclockwise circle in the air after it has left the string. Then, place the bow on the string once again for the second down bow. In this book, circle bows are indicated by a comma (,), also called a breath-mark. Watch the Lesson 12 YouTube tutorial for further instruction on circle bows.

13b: Poppy Sprouts

J. Chimchirian

13c: Sunflower Hop

J. Chimchirian

38

13d: The Pyramid Song with 2nd Finger

J. Chimchirian

"Poppy" on E String

"Poppy" on A String

"Honeysuckle" on E String

"Honeysuckle" on A String

"Sunflower" on E String

"Sunflower" on A String

39

"Rose" on E String

"Rose" on A String

13e: Hummingbird Loves Honeysuckle!

J. Chimchirian

13f: Sunshine and Circle Bows

J. Chimchirian

13g: Giant Sunflowers

J. Chimchirian

SECTION 1 CHALLENGE

Practicing Sight Reading

Sometimes there are situations where it is not possible to practice music ahead of time. **Sight reading** is when music is played for the first time without any prior preparation. You will not be using the 4-step practice method for this challenge. In Challenge 1, try **sight reading** each exercise. Before playing each exercise, take a moment to look at the notes and rhythms so you can be ready for them when it is time to play.

Sight Reading Tip: Even while you are playing, you should look ahead to the next measure to see what is coming next!

Note Reading Challenge 1

Rhythm Challenge 1

Chimchirian

3

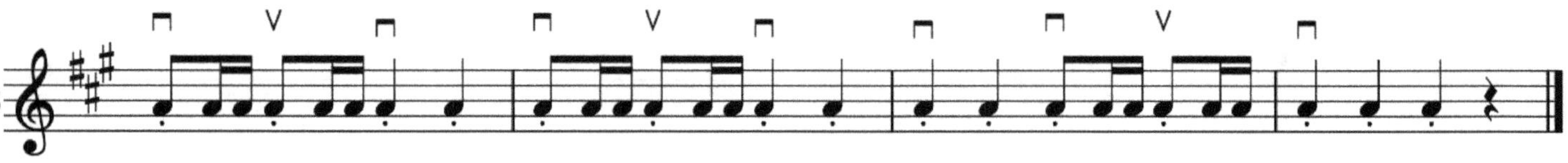

4

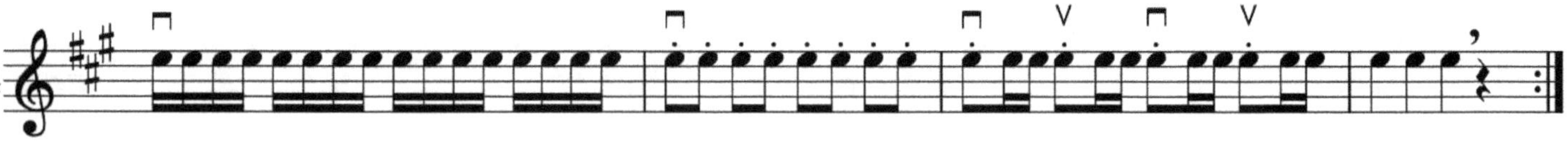

5

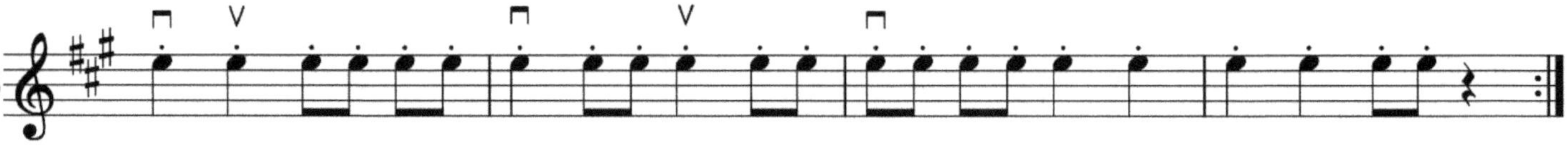

6

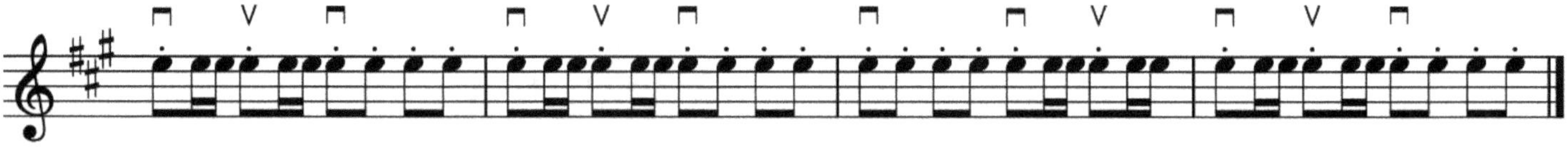

SECTION 2

In this section you will learn the following:

1. How to play and read two new notes by using third finger on both E and A strings

2. How to play and read four new rhythms, including half notes and dotted half notes

3. How to interpret Time Signatures

4. How to play and read songs that combine all these elements

LESSON 14: Flower Garden Rhythms 2

https://youtu.be/0wxcw05l_ME

Learning Rhythms with words

In this lesson, you will learn four flower garden rhythms: **Daffodil, Poppy (rest) And, Half Note** and **1-2-3.** These rhythms are made up of eighth notes, sixteenth notes, half notes and dotted half notes. Scan the QR code beside the Lesson 14 title to watch the tutorial for these new rhythms.

Daffodil

Each Daffodil rhythm is a combination of two **sixteenth notes** and one **eighth note**. Notice how the sixteenth notes have two beams and the eighth note has one beam.

Poppy (rest) And

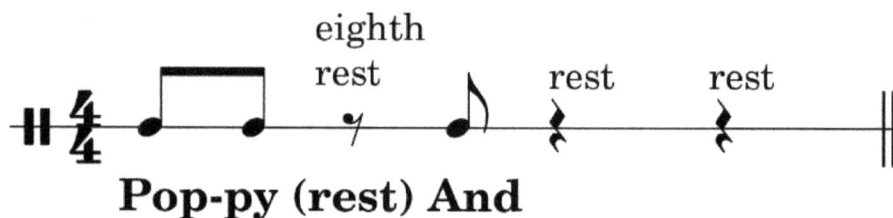

Each Poppy (rest) And rhythm is two **eighth notes**, followed by an **eighth rest**, followed by a single **eighth note**. Notice how the first two eighth notes are beamed together with one beam and how the last single eighth note has a single flag on top. Single eighth notes will always be written with a flag at the top of the stem, so you can easily tell them apart from quarter notes. The rest in between the notes is an eighth rest.

46

Half Note

Half Note = 2 counts

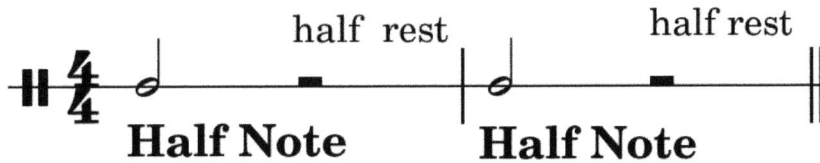

Each Half Note rhythm is one **half note.** A half note is held for two counts and is equal to two quarter notes. A **half rest** is also held for two counts and is equal to two quarter rests.

1-2-3

Dotted Half Note = 3 counts

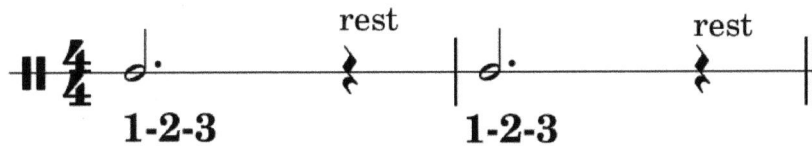

Each 1-2-3 rhythm is a **dotted half note.** A dotted half note is held for three counts and is equal to three quarter notes.

Rests

There are two new rests in this section.

  Eighth Rest = ½ beat

  Half Rest = 2 beats

EXERCISE 14

Practice clapping and saying each of the flower garden rhythms in Lesson 14 until you feel that you have internalized them.

LESSON 15: Playing Flower Garden Rhythms 2

https://youtu.be/VBfsB5w8KtE

Amount of Bow

As you begin to play the rhythms in this section on your open strings, remember to think about how much bow you are using. Scan the QR code beside the Lesson 15 title to watch the tutorial on playing the new rhythms.

The arrows below indicate the amount of bow that should be used for each rhythm. Notice how you will be starting slightly lower than the middle of the bow for the half note and 1-2-3 (dotted half note) rhythms.

1. Daffodil

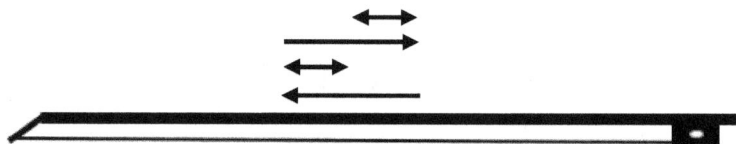

2. Poppy (rest) And

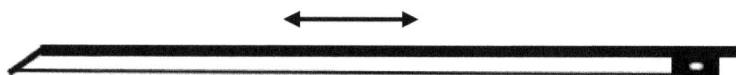

3. Half Note

4. 1-2-3

EXERCISE 15

Play each of the Flower Garden Rhythms 2 in the following exercises. Remember to use an appropriate amount of bow for each rhythm. Work on keeping your bow straight and playing in the middle lane on the string.

48

15. Flower Garden Rhythms 2

Chimchirian 2021

"Daffodil" on E String

"Daffodil" Rock N Roll

"Poppy (rest) And" on E String

"Poppy (rest) And" Rock n' Roll

"Half Note" on E

"Half Note" Rock N Roll

Half Rest = 2 counts

"1-2-3 REST" on E

"1-2-3 REST" Rock N Roll

LESSON 16: The Third Finger

https://youtu.be/IhOZ002NkoY

Playing the Third Finger on A String and E String

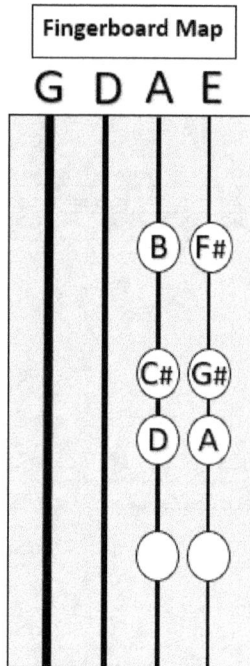

The left-hand ring finger is referred to as the **third finger**. You will use the fingertip of your **third finger** to press down the string in a precise location in order to play two new pitches, D and A. Scan the QR code beside the Lesson 16 title to watch the tutorial on using the third finger.

D	A
is played with third finger on A string, or 3 on A	is played with third finger on E string, or 3 on E

Reading Third Finger on A String and E String

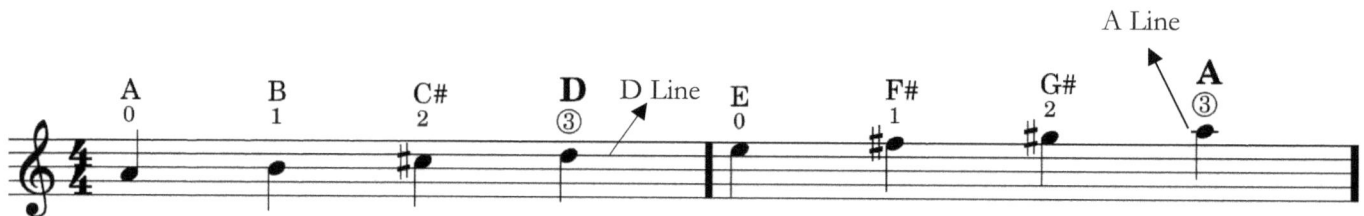

When viewing the music written above, notice how each of these third finger notes fall on a line. **D** is on the second line from the top of the staff, or the line just above the space for C#, indicating that it is one step higher. The same happens for **A**: it occupies the line above the staff, just above the G# space. Lines that are added above or below the staff are called **ledger lines**. Notice how A is on a ledger line.

While playing the following flower garden rhythms, practice pressing down the first finger on E string to make F#, and then the second finger to make G#, then the third finger to make **A.** On A string, practice pressing down the first finger to make B, then the second finger to make C#, and the third finger to make **D**. To learn what A and D sound like, watch the Lesson 16 tutorial. Listen carefully and adjust the placement of your fingertip if you are not playing in tune.

16. The Pyramid Song with 3rd Finger

"Poppy REST &" on A String

"Half Note" on E String

"Half Note" on A String

"1-2-3" rest (dotted half-note)
on E String

"1-2-3" rest (dotted half-note)
on A string

LESSON 17: The A Scale

https://youtu.be/BTl-TsM5Grs

Playing One Octave A Scale

The **A scale** is a stepwise sequence of pitches that starts on open A string and ends on third finger on E, which is also called A. When climbing up to the high A, or third finger on E, it is called an **ascending scale**. When coming back down to the open A string, it is called a **descending scale**. Scan the QR code beside the Lesson 17 title to watch the YouTube tutorial for the A scale.

The Octave

Now you know how to play eight different pitches on the violin, including two different A pitches! One using your open A string, and the other using third finger on E. The distance between open A string and third finger on E is eight notes. This interval is called an **Octave.**

The Musical Alphabet

The musical alphabet is only 7 letters long:

A B C D E F G

Once you get the G, simply start over like this: A B C D E F G A B C D E F G A.... and it continues for a very long time!

If you look once more at the music for the A Scale, can you see the alphabet?

53

Practice playing one octave A scale with each of the flower garden rhythms from Section 1. Pause after each exercise and repeat for a total of five times. To hear what the one octave A scale sounds like, watch the Lesson 17 tutorial.

17. The A Scale (Part 1)

3 "Sunflower"

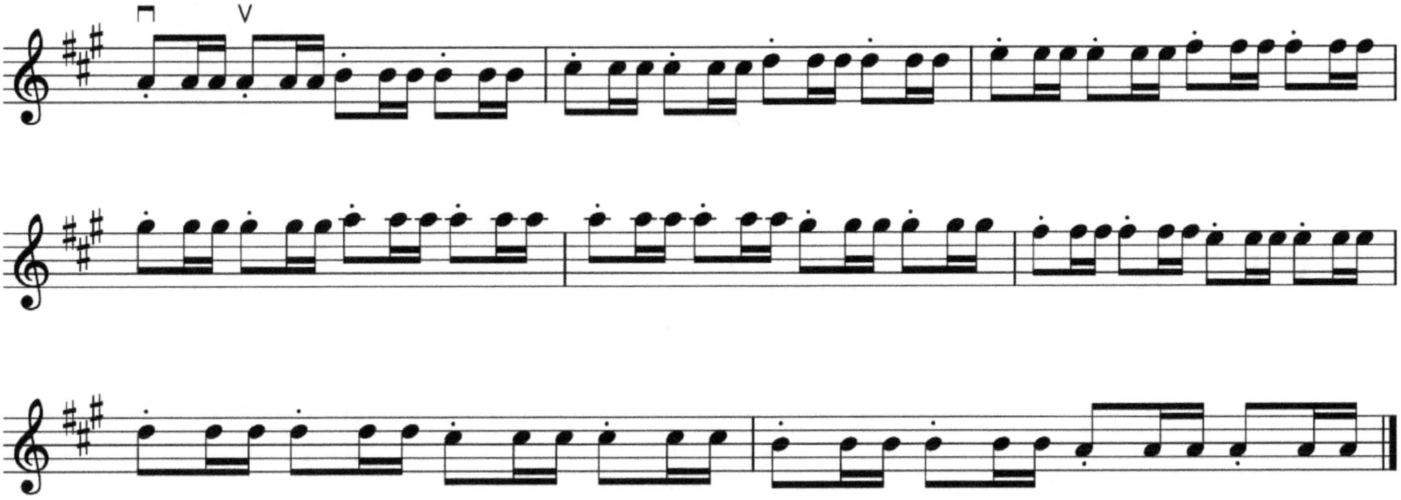

4 "Rose"

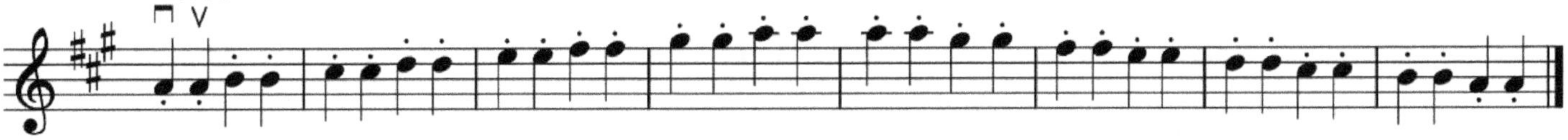

LESSON 18: Time Signatures

https://youtu.be/8cpi7AWmXW8

Understanding Four-Four, Three-Four and Two-Four Time Signatures

The **Time Signature** is a set of two numbers listed at the beginning of a piece of music that organizes it into basic units called measures or bars. The top number determines how many beats are in each bar, and the bottom number indicates what kind of note (quarter, half, eighth, sixteenth) acts as the beat. In this book, we will look at three Time Signatures that use quarter notes as the main metric unit: four-four, three four and two-four. Scan the QR code beside the Lesson 18 title to watch the lesson on Time Signatures.

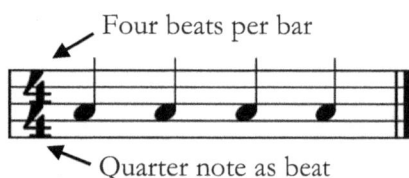

Four-Four Time Signature means the following:
Four beats per bar
Quarter note gets the beat

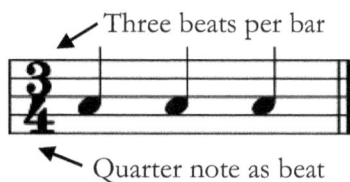

Three-Four Time Signature means the following:
Three beats per bar
Quarter note gets the beat

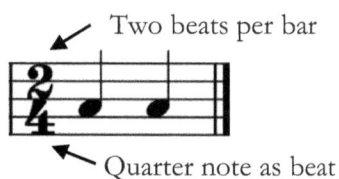

Two-Four Time Signature means the following:
Two beats per bar
Quarter note gets the beat

The following three examples use the same rhythm, first in four-four time, then in three-four time, and finally in two-four time. The placement of the bar lines (or measure lines) change based on the time signature. All three of these examples will sound the same, but the metric feel will be altered based on the changing of the Time Signature.

This is a bar line (also called a measure line)

Make sure to check the Time Signature in the songs coming up at the end of Section 2.

It's time to play some songs with 1st, 2nd and 3rd finger!

https://youtu.be/w2Dx_F32La0

EXERCISE 19

Scan the QR code beside the Lesson 19 title to watch the tutorial for Old MacDonald Had a Farm. You can also use the 4-step practice method to learn this song.

---

19. Old MacDonald Had a Farm

Traditional Arr. Chimchirian

https://youtu.be/kIZoq4xLTmA

EXERCISE 20

Scan the QR code beside the Lesson 20 title to watch the tutorial for Daffodils in Bloom.
You can also use the 4-step practice method to learn this song.

---

20. Daffodils in Bloom

J. Chimchirian

https://youtu.be/SvxfYQ2SbxM

Scan the QR code beside the Lesson 21 title to listen to a recording of the following songs. Use the 4-Step Practice Method from Lesson 7 to learn the songs in Lesson 21.

21a. Poppy Waltz

J. Chimchirian

21b. Twinkle, Twinkle Little Star

Mozart Arr. Chimchirian

21c. Sleepy Squirrel

J. Chimchirian

21d. Bile Em Cabbage Down

Traditional Fiddle arr. Chimchirian

21e. A Scale (Part 2)

J. Chimchirian

62

"Poppy (rest) And"

"Half Note"

"1-2-3"

Notice that there are now 3 beats per measure!

21f. Walking in the Garden

J. Chimchirian

21g. At Pierrot's Door

Traditional Arr. Chimchirian

21h. Yellow Flowers

J. Chimchirian

SECTION 2 CHALLENGE

Practicing Sight Reading

In Section 2 Challenge, try sight reading each exercise. Before playing each exercise, take a moment to look at the notes and rhythms so you can be ready when it is time to play. After the initial sight reading of each line, continue to practice each line until you can play it smoothly.

Sight Reading Tip: Even while you are playing, you should try to look ahead to the next measure to see what is coming up!

Note Reading Challenge 2

Chimchirian

Rhythm Challenge 2

Chimchirian

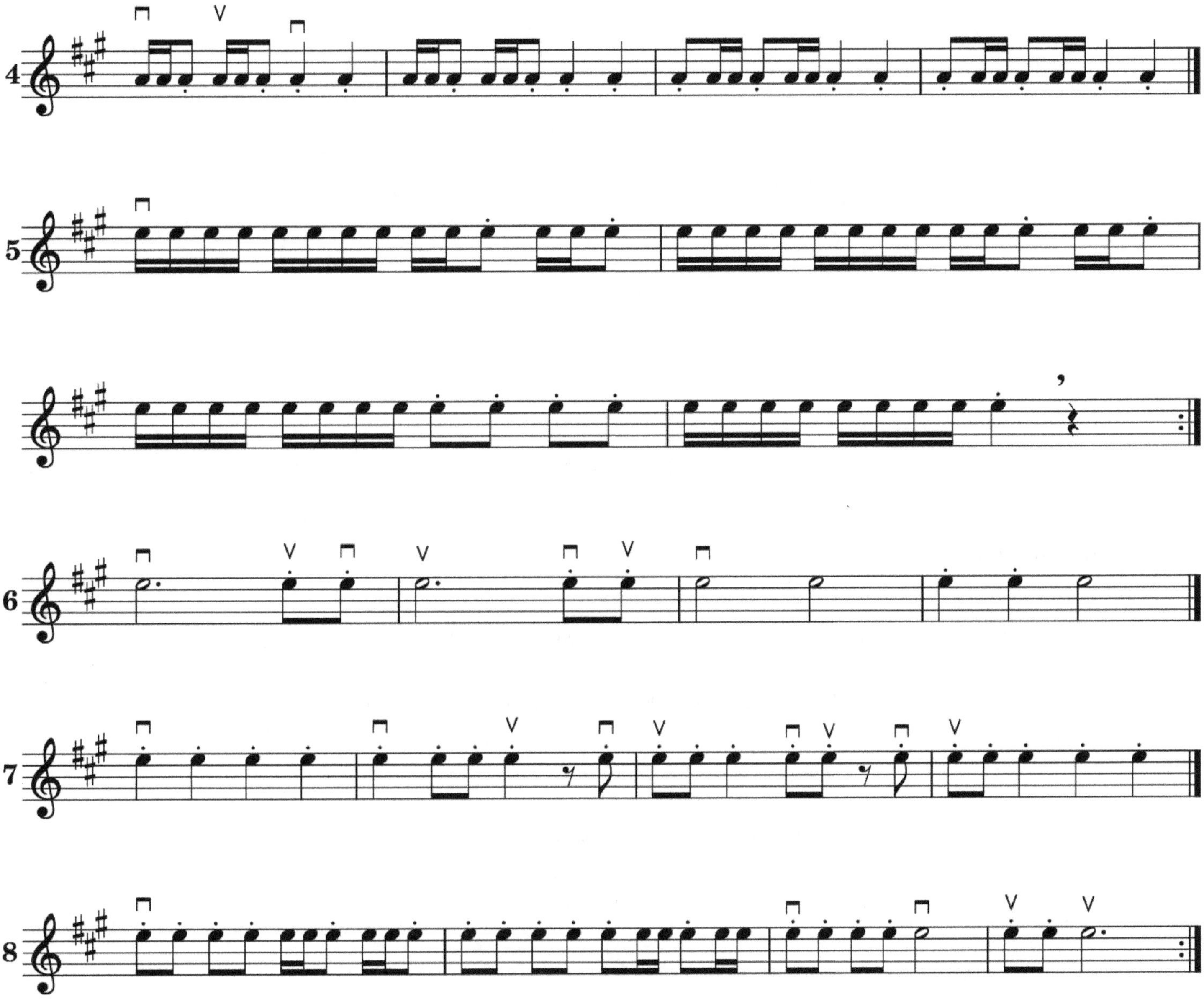
4
5
6
7
8

SECTION 3

In this section you will learn the following:

1. How to play and read two new notes by using fourth finger on both E and A strings

2. How to play and read three new rhythms: Marigold, Iris and Lily

3. An introduction to dynamics and articulations

4. How to play and read songs that combine all these elements

LESSON 22: Flower Garden Rhythms 3

https://youtu.be/9TOD4AZRcZ4

Learning Rhythms with words

In this lesson, you will learn three flower garden rhythms: **Marigold, Iris** and **Lily.** These rhythms are made up of triplet eighth notes, dotted quarter notes and single eighth notes. Scan the QR code beside the lesson 22 title to watch the tutorial for these new rhythms.

Marigold

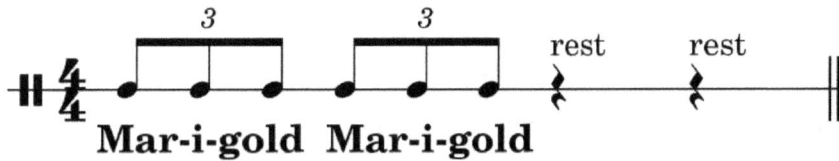

Each Marigold rhythm is three **triplet eighth notes**. Notice how there are 3 **eighth notes** connected by 1 beam. The number 3 is written above **triplet eighth notes** so that you can tell them apart from regular duple (poppy) eighth notes.

Iris

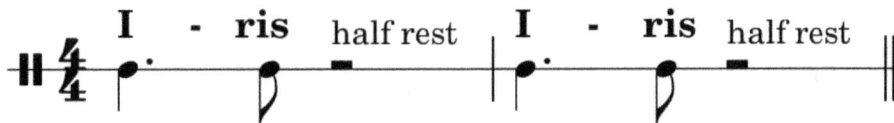

Each Iris rhythm is **1 dotted quarter note** followed by **1 eighth note**. Notice how the single eighth note has a flag at the end of the stem. The dotted quarter note is written with a dot on the right side of the quarter note.

Lily

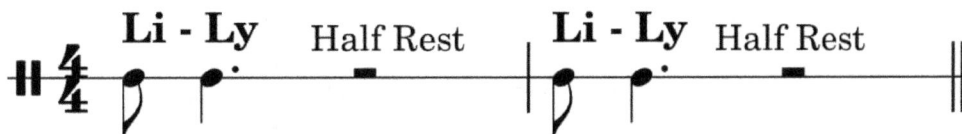

Each Lily rhythm is **one eighth note** followed by **1 dotted quarter note**.

71

The Dotted Quarter Note

Adding a dot to a note increases it's duration by one half. Remember that 1 quarter note is one beat and is equal to two eighth notes.

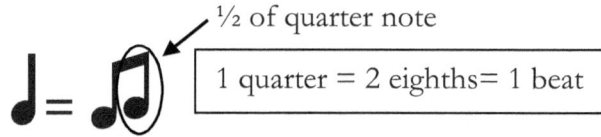

½ of quarter note

1 quarter = 2 eighths= 1 beat

One dotted quarter note is one and a half beats, and is equal to one quarter note plus one eighth note, OR three eighth notes.

½ of quarter

1 dotted quarter = 1 quarter + 1 eighth   Or   1 dotted quarter = 3 eighths

Subdivision is a technique that helps musicians count more complex rhythms like the dotted quarter note. When using the subdivision technique, larger rhythms are divided into their smaller counterparts to ensure rhythmic accuracy. Dotted rhythms like Iris and Lily involve the use of **syncopation**, or playing on the offbeat. In this case, offbeats exist on the second eighth note of each quarter note beat. See the following example for clarification about different ways to subdivide dotted quarter notes for the Iris rhythm. It is helpful to practice keeping track of the eighth notes that comprise the dotted quarter note by using the subdivision technique.

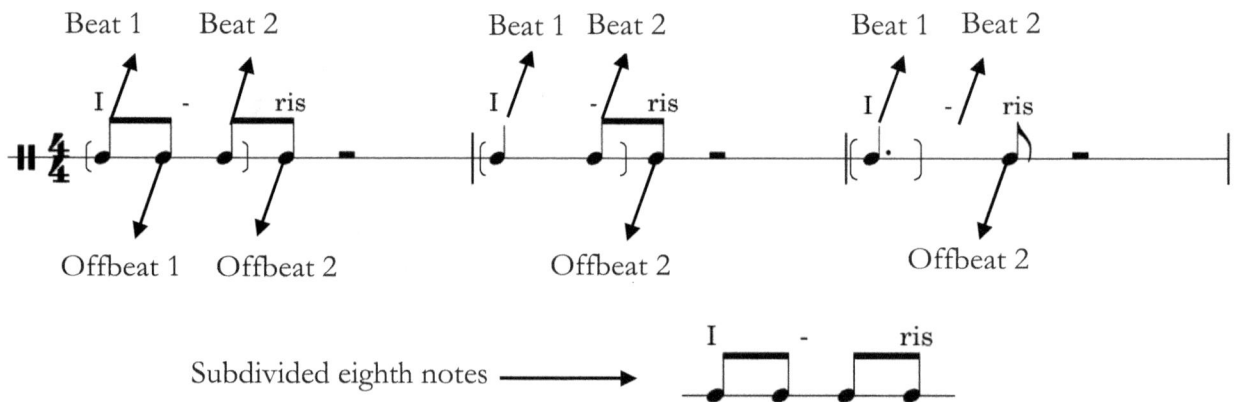

EXERCISE 22.1

Practice clapping and saying each of these rhythms until
you feel that you have internalized them.

Playing Flower Garden Rhythms 3

Amount of Bow

As you begin to play these rhythms on your open strings, remember to think about how much bow you are using. The arrows below indicate the amount of bow that should be used for each rhythm. Scan the QR code below the Lesson 22 title for a tutorial on how to play these rhythms on the violin.

1. **Marigold**

2. **Iris**

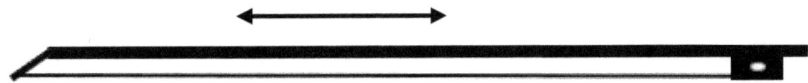

3. **Lily**

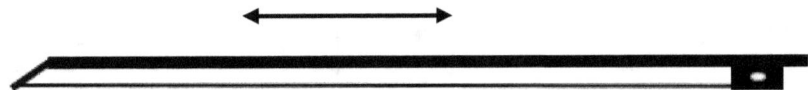

Compensating for Uneven Rhythms

Uneven rhythms, like Iris and Lily, include a long note that alternates with a short note. Playing uneven rhythms on the violin requires a change in bow speed. The long note, in this case a dotted quarter note, should be played with a slower bow speed, and the following short note, the single eighth note, will be played with a fast bow speed. Ideally, both the slow bow and the fast bow should use the same amount of bow (as seen in the diagrams above). Failure to adjust bow speed in cases of uneven bowing can lead to getting stuck at the tip or the frog.

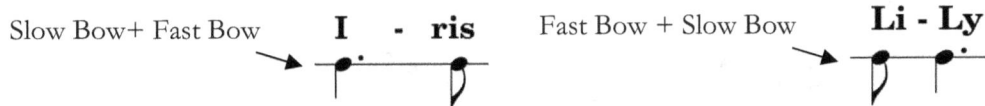

EXERCISE 22.2

Practice playing each of the flower garden rhythms on the E string and A string. Repeat until smooth.

22.2 Flower Garden Rhythms 3

"Marigold" on E String

"Marigold" Rock n' Roll

"Iris" on E String

"Iris" on Rock n' Roll

"Lily" on E String

Make sure you start with an UP bow!

"Lily" Rock n' Roll

LESSON 23: The Fourth Finger

https://youtu.be/Ei5DLtF_9iQ

Playing the Fourth Finger on A String and E String

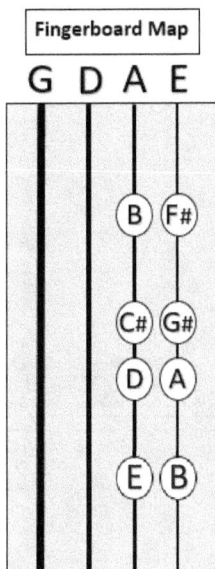

Fingerboard Map

G D A E

The left-hand pinky finger is referred to as the **fourth finger**. You will use the fingertip of your **pinky finger** to press down the string in a precise location in order to play two new notes: E and B. Scan the QR code beside the Lesson 23 title to watch the tutorial on playing with the fourth finger.

E
is played with fourth finger on A string, or 4 on A

B
is played with fourth finger on E string, or 4 on E

Reading Fourth Finger on A String and E String

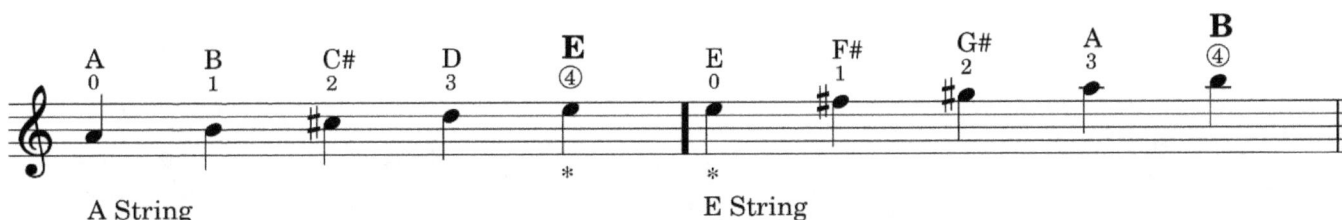

A String   E String

*Notice how you can now play E with either your open E OR with 4th finger on A

When viewing the music above, notice how each of these fourth finger notes fall in a space. **E** is in the top space of the staff, or the space just above the line for D, indicating that it is one step higher. Now it is possible for you to play this E with either the fourth finger on the A string, or the open E string. The same happens for **B**: it occupies the second space above the staff, just above the A ledger line.

While playing the flower garden rhythms, practice putting down all four fingers on both the A string and E string. To learn what the fourth finger on A and E sounds like, watch the Lesson 23 tutorial. Listen carefully and adjust the placement of your fingertip if you are not playing in tune.

23. The Ladder Song

Chimchirian

"Iris" on E String

"Iris" on A String

"Lily" on E String

Make sure you start with an UP bow!

"Lily" on A String

LESSON 24: Dynamics and Articulations

https://youtu.be/DUFmrdpTE_M

Dynamics

Dynamics indicate whether music should be played loudly or quietly. ***Piano*** means to play quietly, and ***forte*** means to play loudly. When playing dynamics, it can be helpful to consider the amount of bow used and the pressure of the bow on the string. *Piano* dynamics can often be achieved by using less bow with a lighter pressure. *Forte* dynamics occur when the player uses longer bow strokes and heavier pressure of the bow on the string. Scan the QR code beside the Lesson 24 title to watch the tutorial on dynamics and articulations.

$\boldsymbol{f}$ *Forte* = Play Loudly $\boldsymbol{p}$ *Piano* = Play Quietly

Gradual changes in dynamics are made by using a **crescendo**, which means to get louder, or **decrescendo**, which means to get softer.

Articulations

Staccato, **Detaché** and **Accents** are different kinds of articulations. Articulations indicate subtle changes in the character of a note regarding the attack, decay, and duration.

Staccato: Play each note short by stopping the bow after each bow stroke. Dots below or above the notehead indicate staccato.

Detaché: Default separated bow stoke. Keep bow moving smoothly until the next bow stroke.

Accent: At the beginning of the stroke, play with a sharp attack by moving the bow quickly and suddenly, then allow the bow speed to slow which causes the sound to relax. Arrows marked below or above the notehead indicate accents.

24a. Hot Cross Buns Staccato with Dynamics

24b. Hot Cross Buns Detaché

24c. Hot Cross Buns with Accents

https://youtu.be/fvkBn_Uo_5A

EXERCISE 25

Scan the QR code beside the Lesson 25 title to watch the tutorial for Ode to Joy.
You can also use the 4-step practice method to learn this song.

---

25. Ode to Joy

Beethoven arr. Chimchirian

https://youtu.be/Fa2b-ooZ4lE

26. Drunken Sailor

Traditional Arr. Chimchirian

LESSON 27: Songs with First, Second, Third and Fourth Fingers

https://youtu.be/_eItGmoEpQ8

> Scan the QR code beside the Lesson 27 title to hear a recording of the songs in Lesson 27. Use the 4-step practice method from Lesson 7 to learn the songs on your own.

27a. Iris Dance

J. Chimchirian

27b. The Ladder Song on E String

J. Chimchirian

"Daffodil"

"Poppy REST &"

84

Half Note"

"1-2-3'

Notice the time signature has changed!

27c. Jingle Bells

Traditional arr. Chimchirian

27d. The A Scale Part 3

J. Chimchirian

"Lily"

27e. This Little Light of Mine

Loes arr. Chimchirian

This is a whole note!

Hold for 4 beats.

27f. Watch the Marigolds Grow

J. Chimchirian

27g. The Ladder Song on A String

Chimchirian

"Sunflower"

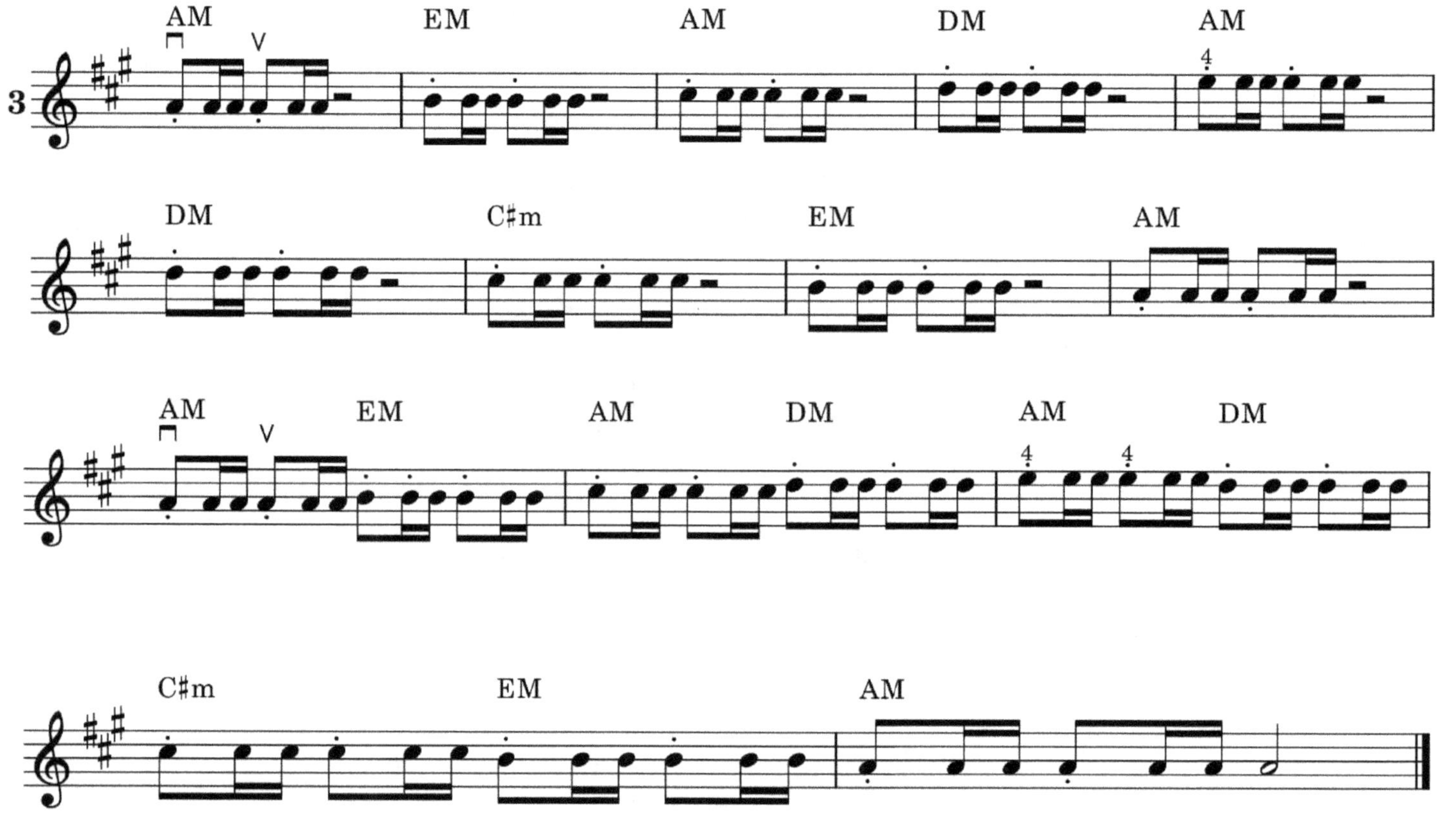

"Rose"

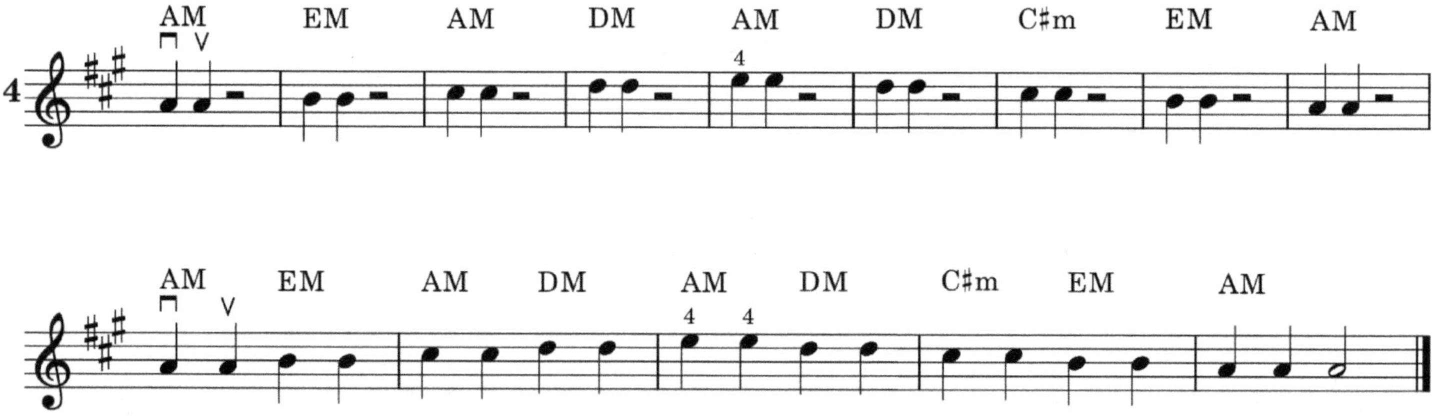

27h. Little Lilies

J. Chimchirian

27i. When the Saints Go Marching In

Traditional arr. Chimchirian

27j. Ladybug Climbs the Honeysuckle

J.Chimchirian

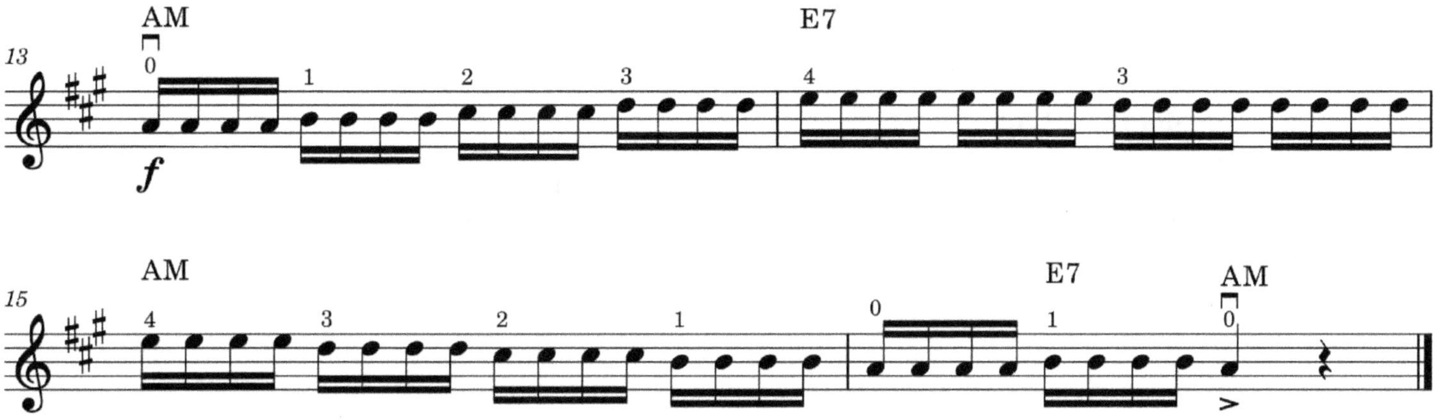
13
AM
0 1 2 3
f
E7
4 3
15
AM
4 3 2 1
0
E7
1
AM
0

SECTION 3 CHALLENGE

Practicing Sight Reading

In Section 3 Challenge, try sight reading each exercise. Before playing each exercise, take a moment to study the notes and rhythms. Once you have looked over the exercises, try playing the entire line with a steady tempo without stopping, even if you make a mistake. After practicing sight reading the exercise, repeat it as many times as necessary until you can play it smoothly, without errors and hesitations.

Sight Reading Tip: Even while you are playing, try to look ahead to the next measure to see what is coming up!

Note Reading Challenge 3

Chimchirian

Rhythm Challenge 3

Chimchirian

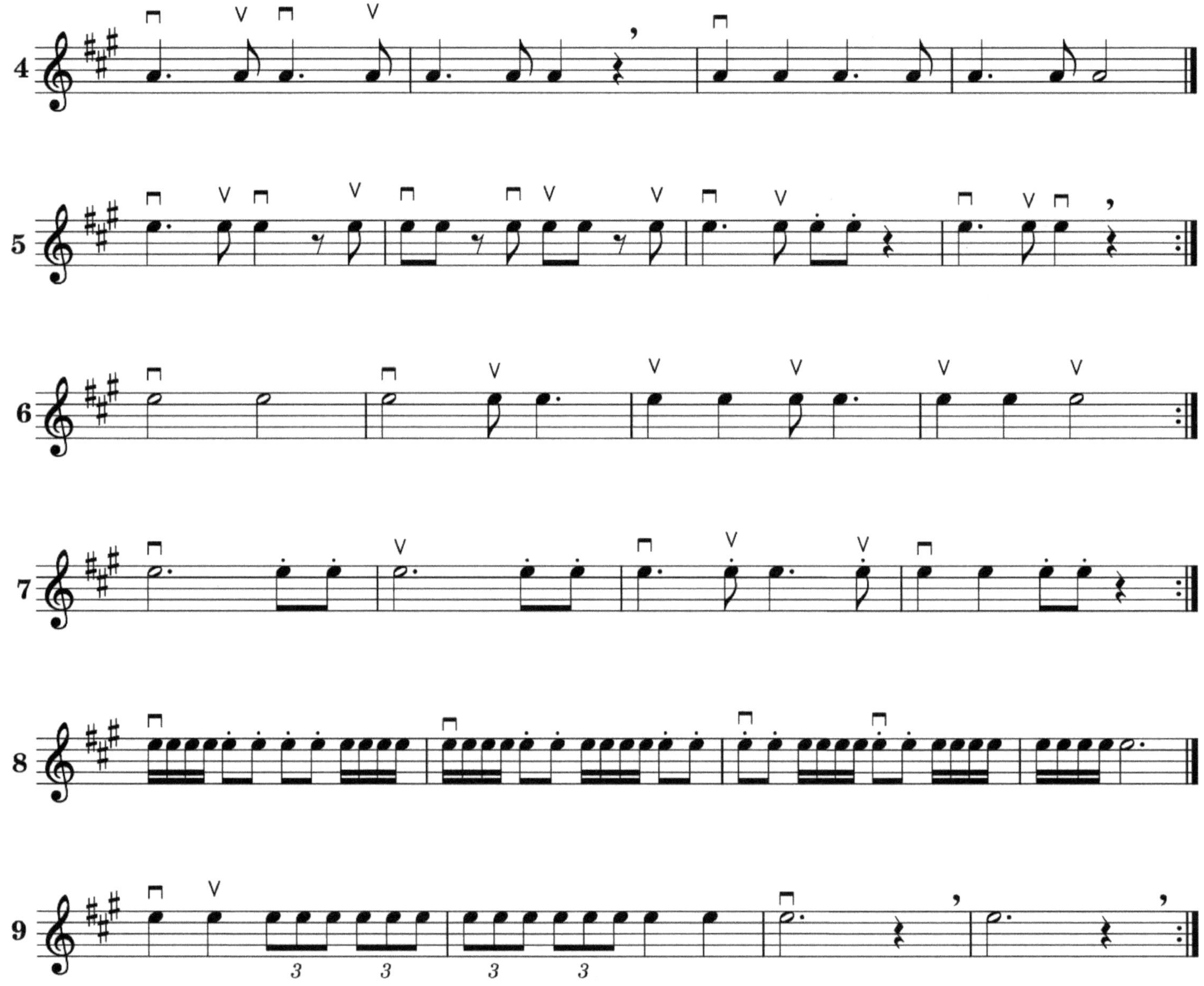
4
5
6
7
8
9
3 3 3 3

www.ingramcontent.com/pod-product-compliance
Lightning Source LLC
LaVergne TN
LVHW081334060426

835513LV00014B/1282